YUMMY VEGAN COOKBOOK

Foolproof Vegan Recipes for Breakfast, Lunch, Dinner, and In-Between

BY

ANNA PARKER

document, including, but not limited to, - errors, omissions, or inaccuracies.

TABLE OF CONTENTS

INTRODUCTION

A Vegan diet is wealthy in vegetables, foods grown from the ground all components of a sound eating routine. The essential contrast between the Vegan diet and other sound eating regimens is the nonappearance of entire grains and vegetables, which are viewed as acceptable wellsprings of fibre, nutrients, and different supplements. Additionally, missing from the eating regimen are dairy items, which are acceptable wellsprings of protein and calcium.

These nourishments not exclusively are viewed as sound yet, in addition, are commonly more moderate and open than such nourishments as wild game, grass-bolstered creatures, and nuts. For specific individuals, a Vegan diet might be excessively costly

Scientists have contended that the fundamental theory of the Vegan diet may distort the narrative of how people adjusted to changes in diet. Contentions for a progressively perplexing comprehension of the advancement of wholesome human needs incorporate the accompanying:

Varieties in diet-dependent on geology, atmosphere, and nourishment accessibility, not just the progress to cultivating. likewise, would have formed the development of dietary needs

Archaeological research has shown that early human eating regimens may have included wild grains as much as 30,000 years back. a long time before the presentation of cultivating.

SMOKY BEAN AND TEMPEH PATTIES

Yield: 8 patties

Protein content per patty: 10 g

Ingredients

- 1 cup (177 g) cooked cannellini beans 8 ounces (227 g) tempeh
- '¼ cup (91 g) cooked bulgur
- 2 cloves garlic, pressed
- ¼ teaspoons onion powder
- 4 teaspoons (20 ml) liquid smoke

- 4 teaspoons (20 ml) vegan Worcestershire sauce
- 1 teaspoon smoked paprika
- 2 tablespoons (30 g) organic ketchup
- 2 tablespoons (40 g) pure maple syrup
- 2 tablespoons (30 ml) neutral-flavored oil
- 3 tablespoons (45 ml) tamari.'
- ¼ cup (60 g) chickpea flour
- Nonstick cooking spray

Instructions

1. Mash the beans in a large bowl: It's okay if a few small pieces of beans are left. Crumble (do not mash) the tempeh into small pieces on top. Add the bulgur and garlic. In a medium bowl, whisk together the remaining ingredients, except the flour and cooking spray. Stir into the crumbled tempeh preparation. Add the flour and mix until well combined. Chill for 1 hour before shaping into patties.

2. Preheat the oven to 350°F (180°C. or gas mark 4). Line a baking sheet with parchment paper. Scoop out a packed 1/3 cup (96 g) per patty, shaping into an approximately 3-inch (8 cm) circle and flattening slightly on the prepared sheet. You should get eight 3.5-inch (9 cm) patties in all. Lightly coat the top of the patties with cooking spray. Bake for 15 minutes, carefully flip, lightly coat the top of the patties with cooking spray, and bake for another 15 minutes until lightly browned and firm.

3. Leftovers can be stored in an airtight container in the refrigerator for up to 4 days. The patties can also be frozen, tightly wrapped in foil, for up to 3 months.

4. If you don't eat all the patties at once, reheat the leftovers on low heat in a skillet lightly greased with

olive oil or cooking spray for about 5 minutes on each side until heated through.

SLOPPY JOE SCRAMBLE STUFFED SPUDS

Yield: 6 potato halves

Protein content per potato half: 12 g

Ingredients

- 1 to 2 tablespoons (15 to 30 ml) high heat neutral-flavored oil
- 1 pound (454 g) extra-firm tofu, drained, pressed, and crumbled
- ¼ teaspoon fine sea salt

- ¼ teaspoon ground black pepper
- ¾ cup (120 g) minced onion
- '¼ cup (75 g) minced bell pepper (any color)
- 3 cloves garlic, minced
- 1 tablespoon (7 g) ground cumin
- 2 teaspoons chili powder, or to taste
- 1 can (15 ounces, or 425 ml) tomato sauce
- 2 tablespoons (30 g) organic ketchup 1 tablespoon (15 ml) tamari
- 1 tablespoon (15 ml) vegan Worcestershire sauce
- 1 tablespoon (11 g) prepared yellow mustard
- 1 (4-inch or 10 cm) dill pickle, minced
- ¾ cup (180 ml) water
- 3 baked potatoes, cooled
- 1 tablespoon (15 ml) olive oil

Instructions

1. Heat 1 tablespoon (15 ml) of oil in a large skillet over medium-high heat. If the skillet is not well-seasoned, add the remaining tablespoon (15 ml) of oil. Add the tofu, salt, and pepper. Cook for 8 to 10 minutes, occasionally stirring until the tofu is firm and golden. Stir in the onion, bell pepper, garlic, cumin, and chili powder. Reduce the heat to medium and cook for 3 minutes, occasionally stirring, until fragrant. Add the

tomato sauce, ketchup, tamari, Worcestershire sauce, mustard, and dill pickle. Bring to a boil, and then reduce the heat to simmer. Swish the water in the tomato sauce can to clean the sides. Simmer for 30 minutes, occasionally stirring, adding the water from the tomato sauce can. As needed for the desired consistency.

2. Preheat the oven to broil. Cut the baked potatoes in half lengthwise. Scoop the insides from the potatoes, leaving about 1 inch (1.3 cm) of the skin intact. Brush both the insides and the outsides of the potato skins with the olive oil and place them on a baking sheet. Broil for 3 to 4 minutes until lightly browned. Remove from the oven and divide the filling evenly in the potatoes, using about ¼ cup (130 g) in each.

SEED CRACKERS

Yield: About 100 crackers, or 20 servings Protein content per serving: 2 g

Ingredients

- 3 tablespoons (36 g) white chia seeds
- ⅓ cup (80 ml) water, more if needed
- 1/3 cup (120 g) packed cooked and cooled amaranth
- ⅓ cup plus 2 tablespoons (75 g) whole wheat pastry flour, plus extra for rolling
- 3 tablespoons (30 g) shelled hemp seeds
- 3 tablespoons (23 g) golden roasted flaxseeds

- 2 tablespoons (15 g) almond meal
- 1½ teaspoons nutritional yeast Generous
- ⅓ teaspoon fine sea salt
- 2 tablespoons (30 ml) olive oil

Instructions

1. Combine the chia seeds with the water in a small bowl. Let stand 2 minutes to thicken.

2. Add flour, flour, hemp seeds, flaxseed, almond flour, yeast, and salt. Add the thick mixture of chia and oil on top. Use a stand mixer with flat blade joints to mix perfectly. If the dough is crushed or dried, add additional water at the same time, a few drops. The mixture should be collected as a very sticky ball. Form the dough into a 5-inch (13 cm) disk. Wrap the dough tightly in a plastic wrap and refrigerate for 2 hours or overnight.

3. Heat the oven to 400 degrees Fahrenheit (200 degrees Celsius or gas mark 6). Draw two large baking sheets with enamel paper. Divide the dough into 4 parts.

4. Put a quarter of the dough on a piece of soft paper wrapped in flour, sprinkle the mixture with a little flour and cover it almost thin, almost! 4 ⁺ inches (1.6 mm). Using a 2-inch (5 cm) round cutter, cut the dough into cookies and transfer it to prepared slices.

Dissolve the remaining mixture until it is finished and repeat the dough for another 3 quarts. You can also wrap the remaining dough well and put it back in the refrigerator for later use for 4 days.

5. Cook for 8 minutes and check the softness: cracks should be browned everywhere. Some cookies are likely to bake faster than others. Take the ones that are ready and move them to a wire rack. Bake for another minute, until well cooked until lightly browned. Allow cooling on a rack before stacking in an airtight container at room temperature. You must enjoy the rest for 2 days.

SPELT AND SEED ROLLS

Yield: 9 rolls

Protein content per roll: 15 g

- Ingredients
- 1 cup (235 ml) unsweetened plain vegan milk, lukewarm
- 2 teaspoons apple cider vinegar
- ⅓ cup (120 ml) water, lukewarm
- 2 tablespoons (30 ml) neutral-flavored oil
- 2 tablespoons (40 g) agave nectar
- 3 cups plus scant
- ⅓ cup (480 g) whole spelt flour, divided
- ¼ cup (30 g) oat flour or finely ground oats
- ¼ cup (36 g) vital wheat gluten
- 3 tablespoons (30 g) shelled hemp seeds
- 3 tablespoons (25 g) sunflower seeds
- 2 tablespoons (15 g) golden roasted flaxseeds
- 2 tablespoons (24 g) chia seeds
- 1 tablespoon (7 g) caraway seeds or (9 g) poppy seeds
- 1 teaspoon fine sea salt
- 2 teaspoons instant yeast

Instructions

1. Combine milk and vinegar in a measuring cup. Allow two minutes to milk. This is your "license."

2. Add water, oil and agave (or maple syrup or molasses) to the butter. Set aside.

3. In a bowl, place a 3A cup (450 g) of ground flour, oatmeal, wheat gluten, whole grains, salt, and yeast. Pour the wet ingredients over the dry ones.

4. Knead the dough with a stand mixer for 10 minutes until the dough becomes soft and not too dry or too sticky. If necessary, gently add 1 tablespoon (15 ml).

5. Cover for 75 minutes or until doubled.

6. Hit the dough. Place on a soft baking sheet, lightly smooth and form a circular disk approximately 10 inches (25 cm) long. Cover both sides of the disc with flour. Make 9 equal triangles from the center, similar to the buns. You can shape them or put them in round loaves.

7. Slowly sprinkle the extra flour and place it back on a baking sheet. Slowly lower by pressing the palm of your hand. Cover with plastic wrap. Let it grow for 25 minutes.

8. While the rolls rise, heat the oven to 400 degrees Fahrenheit (200 degrees Celsius, or gas mark 6). Remove the plastic wrap and do not brown or hollow

it for 20 to 22 minutes or until it touches the bottom of the roll. Let cool on a rack. Store the rest in an airtight container at room temperature. Roulette is best enjoyed fresh, but it will last up to 2 days.

NUT AND SEED SPRINKLES

Yield: 2 cups (225 g), or 32 servings

Protein content per serving: 2 g

Ingredients

- 1 cup (145 g) toasted whole almonds
- ¼ cup plus 2 tablespoons (45 g) nutritional yeast
- ¼ cup (40 g) shelled hemp seeds

- 1 teaspoon white miso, or scant ½ teaspoon fine sea salt, to taste
- 1 to 2 cloves garlic, grated or pressed, to taste
- 1½ teaspoons favorite dried herb, or a blend (dried basil, dried oregano, etc.), optional
- '¼ teaspoon cayenne pepper, or to taste, optional

Instructions

1. Place all the ingredients in a food processor. Pulse to combine until the almonds are coarsely ground to the consistency of panko bread crumbs.
2. Store in an airtight container in the refrigerator for up to 2 weeks.

ALMOND OR CASHEW BISCUITS

Yield: 9 biscuits

Protein content for cookie: 15 g

Ingredients

- 1¼ cups (150 g) whole wheat pastry flour or (156 g) all-purpose flour
- ⅓ cup (47 g) toasted whole cashews or (48 g) almonds (Use unsalted.)
- ½ teaspoon fine sea salt
- 1½ teaspoons baking powder
- 1 tablespoon (42 g) semi-solid coconut oil (the texture of softened butter)
- 3 tablespoons (48 g) natural smooth cashew butter or almond butter
- ½ cup (120 g) blended soft silken tofu or unsweetened plain vegan yogurt

Instructions

1. Preheat the oven to 425°F (220°C, or gas mark 7). Line a baking sheet with parchment paper.
2. Place the flour and nuts in a food processor. Pulse until the nuts are chopped: ¼ few larger pieces are okay.

Add the salt and baking powder and pulse a couple of times.

3. Add the oil and nut butter and pulse to combine. Add the blended tofu or yogurt, and pulse until a crumbly (but not dry) dough forms. Gather the dough on a piece of parchment and pat it together to shape into a 6-inch (15 cm) square.

4. Cut into nine 2-inch (5 cm) square biscuits. Transfer the cookies to the prepared baking sheet. Bake for 12 to 14 minutes, or until golden brown at the edges cool on a wire rack and serve.

MUSHROOM CASHEW MINI PIES

Yield: 24 mini pies

Protein content for cake: 2 g

Ingredients

For the filling:

- 1 scant cup (210 g) Creamy Cashew Baking Spread
- 1/3 cup (80 g) minced rehydrated dried mushrooms of choice
- ¼ cup (15 g) chopped fresh parsley
- 2 tablespoons (20 g) minced red onion
- 2 tablespoons (15 g) nutritional yeast
- 2 cloves garlic, grated or pressed

- ¼ teaspoon fine sea salt
- ¼ teaspoon ground nutmeg Ground black or white pepper

For the crusts:

- Nonstick cooking spray
- 1¼ cups (150 g) whole wheat pastry flour
- ¼ cup (40 g) hemp powder
- Scant ½ teaspoon fine sea salt
- 2 tablespoons (32 g) cashew butter
- 2 tablespoons (30 ml) neutral-flavored oil
- ¼ cup plus 2 tablespoons (90 ml) cold unsweetened plain vegan milk, as needed

Instructions

1. **To make the filling:** In a medium bowl, combine all the ingredients with a spoon until thoroughly mixed. Set aside while preparing the crusts.

2. **To make the crusts:** Preheat the oven to 350°F (180°C, or gas mark 4). Lightly coat a 24-cup mini muffin pan with cooking spray. Place the flour, hemp powder, and salt in a large bowl. In a small bowl, stir to combine the cashew butter and oil. Using a fork, cut the cashew butter mixture into the flour mixture. Add ¼ cup (60 ml) of the milk, stirring until crumbs form, adding an extra tablespoon (15 ml) at a time if

needed. The crumbs of dough should stick together easily when pinched and be neither too dry, nor too wet.

3. Place a generous 1¼ teaspoons of crumbs in each muffin cup, pressing down to fit the bottom and sides of the bowl. Add 2 generous teaspoons of filling the per crust, smoothing out the tops.

4. Bake for 22 minutes or until the tops are firm and light golden brown. Remove from the pan, transfer to a wire rack, and serve warm or at room temperature. Leftovers can be stored in an airtight container in the refrigerator for up to 2 days and reheated in a 325°F (170°C, or gas mark 3) oven until warm, about 15 minutes.

SAUCE RECIPES

20-MINUTE TOFU SOUP

Yield: 3 to 4 servings

Protein content for serving: 12 g

Ingredients

- 1 tablespoon (15 ml) neutral-flavored oil
- 1 teaspoon toasted sesame oil ¼ cup (53 g) minced shallot
- ¼ cup (40 g) minced garlic
- 2 teaspoons grated fresh ginger root
- 8 ounces (227 g) extra-firm tofu, drained, pressed, cut into skinny slices, then into ½-inch (6 mm) pieces
- ½ cup plus 2 tablespoons (90 g) daikon matchsticks
- 3 tablespoons (43 g) minced carrot ½ teaspoon ground white pepper
- ½ teaspoon cayenne pepper, or to taste
- 2½ cups (590 ml) vegetable broth
- 3 tablespoons (45 ml) tamari
- 2 tablespoons (30 ml) seasoned rice vinegar
- 1 teaspoon to taste Minced scallion, for garnish

Instructions

1. Heat the oils in a medium-size saucepan over medium heat. Add the shallot, garlic, and ginger. Cook for 3 minutes, occasionally stirring, until fragrant.

2. Add the tofu, daikon, carrot, white pepper, and cayenne pepper. Some of the tofu may break, and that is okay. Cook for 2 minutes, stirring.

3. Add the broth, tamari vinegar and sambal oelek. Bring to a boil, and then reduce to a simmer. Cook for 10 minutes serves garnished with scallion.

TEMPEH NOODLE SOUP

This home-style soup has a savory broth with a depth of flavor that showcases the tempeh wonderfully. We love how the texture of the protein-rich tempeh is the ideal counterpoint to the pasta.

Yield: 4 servings

Protein content per serving: 19 g

Ingredients

- 4 ounces (113 g) capellini, angel hair, or other thin pasta

- 8 ounces (227 g) tempeh. simmered, and cut into small cubes
- 2 tablespoons (30 ml) high heat neutral-flavored oil
- 1 medium onion, minced (about 1½cups. or 240 g)
- 2 carrots, chopped (about a cup. or 98 g)
- 1 stalk celery, chopped (about 14 cups. or 60 g)
- 3 cloves garlic, minced
- 1 teaspoon ground cumin
- 1 teaspoon dried mustard
- 1 teaspoon onion powder
- 1 teaspoon dried poultry seasoning
- 1 teaspoon dried thyme
- ¼ teaspoon ground white pepper
- ¼ teaspoon turmeric
- ¼ cup (60 ml) dry white wine, or vegetable broth
- 5 to 6 cups (1.2 to 1.4 L) water
- 2 tablespoons (15 g) nutritional yeast
- 1 tablespoon (18 g) no chicken bouillon paste
- ¼ cup (33 g) frozen peas, thawed 1 tablespoon (4 g) fresh minced parsley
- Salt and pepper

Instructions

1. Bring a medium-size pot of salted water to a boil. Break the capellini into 1-inch (2.5 cm) pieces and

cook al dente according to the package directions. Drain and rinse under cold water. Set aside.

2. Heat the oil in a large soup pot over medium-high heat. Cook the tempeh for 7 to 9 minutes, occasionally stirring, until browned. Transfer to a plate and set aside. Add the onion, carrots, and celery to the soup pot. Cook for 4 to 6 minutes, stirring occasionally. Add the garlic through the turmeric and cook another minute to toast the spices lightly. Add the wine or broth and scrape up any bits from the bottom of the pot. Return the tempeh to the pot and add 5 cups (1.2 L) of water, the nutritional yeast, and bouillon. Bring to a boil, and then reduce the heat to simmer. Add the additional cup (235 ml) of water, if desired. Cook for 20 minutes add the peas and cook for 2 minutes longer. Stir in the noodles and parsley. Taste and adjust the seasonings before serving.

SHISHITO PEPPERS WITH PEANUT-TOFU SAUCE

Yield: About 20 peppers, plus 1 generous cup (300 g) Peanut-Tofu Sauce

Protein content per pepper (with sauce): 33 g

Ingredients

- 6 ounces (170 g) extra-firm silken tofu, drained
- 3 tablespoons (48 g) smooth or chunky peanut butter
- 3 tablespoons (45 ml) seasoned rice vinegar
- 2 tablespoons (30 ml) tamari
- 1 teaspoon garlic powder
- 1 teaspoon onion powder
- ½ teaspoon ginger powder
- 1 to 3 teaspoons (5 to 15 g) sriracha. or to taste
- 2 teaspoons olive oil
- 4 ounces (113 g) shishito peppers (about 20 peppers)
- 2 tablespoons (12 g) minced scallion
- 1 tablespoon (9 g) chopped dry-roasted peanuts
- 2 teaspoons toasted sesame seeds Coarse sea salt, for sprinkling

Instructions

1. Combine the tofu, peanut butter, vinegar, tamari, garlic powder, onion powder, and ginger powder in a small blender. Process until completely smooth. Add sriracha to taste and blend again.

2. Heat the oil in a large skillet over medium-high heat. Cook the peppers for 4 to 6 minutes, occasionally turning, until there are a few black spots and blisters. Transfer to a plate and spoon as much sauce as desired over the peppers, serving some extra on the side. Sprinkle with the scallion, peanuts, sesame seeds, and salt.

SEITAN BOLOGNESE

Yield: 4 servings

Protein content per serving: 47 g

Ingredients

- 12 ounces (340 g) Kind-to-Cows Seitan cutlets
- 2 tablespoons (30 ml) olive oil ¼ cup (80 g) minced onion
- ½ cup (28 g) minced carrot
- ¼ cup (36 g) minced green bell pepper
- 3 tablespoons (22 g) minced celery
- 4 ounces (113 g) cremini mushrooms, minced
- 1 tablespoon (10 g) minced garlic
- ½ teaspoon dried thyme, or 1 ¼ teaspoon fresh
- ½ teaspoon red pepper flakes
- 1 bay leaf
- Pinch of grated nutmeg
- Vs cup (160 ml) dry white wine, or vegetable broth
- 1 can (14.5 ounces, or 411 g) diced fire-roasted tomatoes, undrained
- 3 tablespoons (45 ml) vegetable broth
- 2 tablespoons (32 g) tomato paste
- 1 vegetable bouillon cube

- ¾ cup (180 ml) unsweetened soymilk
- Salt and pepper
- 12 ounces (340 g) flat, wide noodles, cooked

Instructions

1. Tear the seitan cutlets into large pieces. Use a food processor to pulse the pieces into chunks. Try not to process the seitan into a mince, but leave various sizes of fragments from 1-inch (2.5 cm) to smaller. Heat the oil in a large pot over medium-high heat. Add the seitan and cook for 4 to 6 minutes, occasionally stirring, until browned. Some of the seitan will stick to the pot. And that is alright. Add the onion through the nutmeg and cook, stirring for 3 to 5 minutes, until the onion is translucent.

2. Reduce the heat to medium. Add the ⅔ cup (160 ml) wine or broth, scraping any bits from the bottom. Add the tomatoes. 3 tablespoons (45 ml) vegetable broth, tomato paste, and bouillon cube. Lower the heat and simmer the sauce for one hour. While simmering, stir in ¼ cup (60 ml) of soymilk at a time every 15 minutes until all the soymilk is added. Stir occasionally while cooking. Remove the bay leaf and season to taste. Add the noodles to the pot and stir to coat, adding up to 1 cup (235 ml) cooking water if needed to make the mixture saucier.

SEITAN PAPRIKASH

Yield: 4 servings

Protein content per serving: 27 g

Ingredients

- 1 cup (235 ml) water
- ¼ cup (35 g) raw cashews
- 1½ cups (355 ml) vegetable broth, divided
- 1 tablespoon (15 ml) apple cider vinegar
- 1 tablespoon (15 ml) unsweetened plain vegan milk
- 1½ teaspoons fresh lemon juice

- Salt and pepper
- ¼ cup plus 1 tablespoon (50 g) all-purpose flour
- 3 (each 4 ounces, or 113 g) Quit-the- Cluck Seitan cutlets, cut into quarters, or 12 nuggets
- 2 tablespoons (30 ml) high heat neutral-flavored oil
- 1 medium onion, cut into 14-inch (1.3 cm) thick slices
- 1 red bell pepper, cut into 14-inch (6 mm) thick slices
- 4 cloves garlic, minced
- 2 tablespoons (14 g) Hungarian paprika
- ¼ teaspoon caraway seeds, optional
- 3 tablespoons (48 g) tomato paste

Instructions

1. Pour the water to a boil in a small saucepan. Add the boys. Mix the heat in a pan and cook for 10 minutes. Drain and drain in a small and powerful blender and add a teaspoon (60 ml) of broth, vinegar, milk, lemon juice, and salt. Process until completely smooth and reserve.

2. Combine the flour with a handful of salt and pepper on a shallow plate. Sprinkle the flour over the flour to cover it completely. Heat the oil in a large skillet over medium heat. Bake the cyan (batch) for 4-6 minutes to brown. Turn and cook on the other side for 3 to 5 minutes until golden brown. Remove and reserve.

3. Reduce the temperature to medium. Add the onions to the same pan and cut each part of the bottom. Cook for 4-6 minutes until soft. Add the pepper and cook for 3 to 4 minutes. The pepper still needs to be ground. Add the garlic, paprika and cream seeds and cook for 2 minutes and stir. Add the remaining broth (295 ml) and tomato paste. Bring to a boil, then reduce the heat to a boil for 10 to 12 minutes or until it thickens. Add the cheese mixture, stir to combine. Add the potatoes and simmer for 4-6 minutes to heat. Adjust and adjust seasonings. Serve over pasta or grain if desired.

CREAMY CASHEW SAUCE

Yield: Scant 2 cups (440 ml) sauce, or 8 servings

Protein content per serving: 2 g

Ingredients

- 1 cup (140 g) raw cashews (covered with water, soaked 8 hours, drained, rinsed)
- 1 cup (235 ml) vegetable broth
- 1 tablespoon (30 ml) fresh lemon juice
- 1 tablespoon (18 g) white miso
- 1 tablespoon (12 g) cornstarch
- 1 teaspoon onion powder
- Salt and pepper

Instructions

1. Combine all the ingredients in a blender and blend until perfectly smooth. Add to a medium saucepan and cook on medium-low heat until thickened, constantly whisking, about 3 minutes.
2. Remove from the heat and whisk occasionally to avoid having a "skin" form on top of the mixture. Adjust seasoning as needed. Use immediately, or store in an airtight container in the refrigerator for up to 4 days.

CREAMY CASHEW BAKING SPREAD

Yield: 10 ounces (283 g) baking spread

Protein content per serving: 26 g

Ingredients

- 1 cup (140 g) raw cashews (covered with water, soaked 8 hours, drained and rinsed)
- Protein content per serving cup (120 ml) vegetable broth
- 1 tablespoon (15 ml) fresh lemon juice

Instructions

1. Combine the cashews, soup, and lemon juice in a food processor or high-speed blender. Process until thoroughly smooth, stopping to scrape the sides occasionally. This might take up to 10 minutes depending on the efficiency of your food processor or blender.

2. Place in a glass bowl and cover tightly. Leave at room temperature for 24 hours or until the spread smells tangy. This will depend on the temperature of your living area. Store in the refrigerator after that for up to 1 week.

QUICK ENERGY & RECOVERY SNACKS

CASHEW RAITA

Yield: 21 ounces (585 g), or 12 servings

Protein content per serving: 6 g

Ingredients

For the cashew base:

- 1 cup (210 g) raw cashew pieces
- ¼ cup (60 ml) water, plus more to soak cashews, divided
- ¼ cup (60 ml) coconut cream
- 2 tablespoons (30 ml) fresh lemon juice
- Protein content per serving teaspoon fine sea salt

For the raita:

- 1 English hothouse cucumber, cut into 6 large pieces
- 1 recipe cashew base
- 3 tablespoons (5 g) packed fresh mint leaves
- 3 tablespoons (11 g) packed fresh parsley
- 3 tablespoons (3 g) packed fresh cilantro
- 1 to 2 cloves garlic, grated or pressed, to taste
- 1 teaspoon organic lemon zest
- 2 teaspoons to 1 tablespoon (10 to 15 ml) fresh lemon juice
- Fine sea salt

Instructions

1. To make the cashew base: Place the cashews in a medium bowl or four-cup (940 ml) glass measuring cup. Generously cover with water. Cover with plastic wrap, or a lid, and let stand at room temperature overnight (about 8 hours) to soften the nuts.

2. Drain the hips (release the soaking water) and rinse quickly. Put in a high-speed food processor or mixer with a cup (60 ml) of water, coconut cream, lemon juice, and salt. To keep it soft, occasionally scrape the sides with a rubber spatula. This may take up to 10 minutes, depending on the power of the device.

3. Move the dispenser to a medium container covered with a lid or covered with a plastic wrap and let it sit for 24 hours at room temperature or until the smell is stained. It depends on the temperature of your location.

4. To make Rita: Put the cucumber in a pan and press several times until it is crushed. Add the remaining ingredients and press to mix correctly, stopping to crush the sides with a rubber floor once or twice. Adjust seasonings if necessary. Refrigerate for at least 2 hours or overnight to allow the flavors to melt. Refrigerate slowly before serving. The waste can be stored in the refrigerator for up to 4 days.

NO-BAKE CHOCO CASHEW CHEESECAKE

Yield: 8 to 12 servings

Protein content per serving: 9 g

Ingredients

- 2 cups (280 g) raw cashews
- ¼ cup (60 ml) coconut cream
- ¼ cup (20 g) unsweetened cocoa powder
- ¼ cup (160 g) pure maple syrup 1 teaspoon vanilla extract
- 1¼ cups (125 g) walnut halves
- ¼ cup (89 g) chopped dates
- ¼ teaspoon ground cinnamon
- ¼ cup (30 g) almond meal, as needed

Instructions

1. Line the bottom of four 4-inch (10 cm) spring-form pans with a parchment paper circle.

2. Place peanuts, coconut cream, cocoa powder, maple syrup and vanilla in a high-speed food processor or mixer. Repeat the process until it is entirely smooth, occasionally scraping the pieces with a rubber spatula. Depending on the performance of your device, this

may take up to 10 minutes. Transfer the mixture to a medium bowl and set aside. Clean the food processor or blender with a paper towel.

Place the nuts, dates, and cinnamon in the same food processor or high-speed mixer. Mix and chop finely until mixed. Be careful not to over-process or make the mixture too sticky. If it is too late and the dough is too sticky, combine the almond flour. Press on the prepared pot. Put the cheese mixture in the peel and smooth from above. Place the pans in an airtight container for 3 hours and place them in the freezer to dry (this will make them less dirty), remove the cheese from the pots, and put them back in the refrigerator to prepare food.

CACAO-COATED ALMONDS

Yield: 2¼ cups (320 g) almonds, or 10 servings

Protein content per serving: 7 grams

Ingredients

- ¼ cup (35 g) cacao nibs
- ¼ cup (38 g) light brown sugar (not packed)
- 1 teaspoon instant espresso powder, optional
- Pinch of kosher salt
- 2 teaspoons cornstarch 2 teaspoons warm water
- 1 tablespoon (20 g) pure maple syrup
- 1 teaspoon pure vanilla extract
- 2 cups (240 g) roasted whole almonds
- ¼ cup (30 g) powdered sugar, optional

Instructions

1. Preheat the oven to 325°F (170°C, or gas mark 3). Have a large rimmed baking sheet lined with parchment paper handy.
2. Place the cacao nibs, sugar, espresso powder, and salt in a coffee grinder. Grind to turn into a fine powder.
3. In a large bowl, whisk the cornstarch with the warm water until thoroughly combined. Stir the maple syrup

and vanilla into the mixture. Add the almonds on top and fold until thoroughly coated.

4. Add the ground cacao mixture and combine until the almonds are thoroughly coated.

5. Place the almonds evenly on the baking sheet. Toast for 10 minutes remove from the oven and stir gently. Toast for another 5 minutes or until the coating looks mostly dry. Be careful not to allow to burn!

6. Let cool on the sheet. The coating will further harden once cooled. Once completely cooled, place the nuts in a bowl or Ziploc bag and dust with the sugar, shaking to coat thoroughly. Store in an airtight container in the refrigerator for up to 2 weeks.

DO THE COCOA SHAKE

Yield: 4 servings, 1 cup (235 ml) per serving

Protein content per serving: 11 g

Ingredients

- 12 ounces (340 g) soft silken tofu
- 1 (355 ml) unsweetened plain or vanilla vegan milk of choice
- ¼ cup (80 g) agave nectar or pure maple syrup, adjust to taste
- ¼ cup (64 g) natural creamy peanut or almond butter, slightly salted is fine
- ¼ cup (20 g) unsweetened cocoa powder
- 1 teaspoon pure vanilla extract
- 2 tablespoons (20 g) hemp powder, optional
- 1 frozen banana (peeled before freezing in a plastic sandwich bag), optional
- Ice cubes, optional

Instructions

1. Combine all the ingredients in a blender and blend until perfectly smooth. Add hemp powder for an extra boost of protein, a sliced frozen banana for a thicker and fruitier shake, or ice cubes for a colder, thicker

shake without any added flavor. Serve immediately or refrigerate for later use: be sure to only add the ice cubes upon serving, if storing for later. Stir well or blend again if adding ice cubes.

TEMPEH KOFTAS WITH CASHEW DIP

Yield: 20 koftas. plus 1 scant cup (230 g) dip

Protein content per kofta (with sauce): 6 g

For the simple cashew dip:

- ¾ cup (180 g) cashew base
- 1½ tablespoons (6 g) packed minced fresh parsley
- 1 ¼ tablespoon (23 ml) fresh lemon juice
- 1½ tablespoons (24 g) tahini
- 1 to 2 cloves garlic, grated or pressed, to taste
- Salt and pepper

For the koftas:

- Nonstick cooking spray
- 1 cup (177 g) cannellini beans or 1 cup (171 g) black-eyed peas
- 8 ounces (227 g) tempeh
- ¾ cup (40 g) minced red onion
- ¾ cup (16 g) packed flat-leaf parsley, minced
- 2 tablespoons (30 ml) neutral-flavored oil, plus extra for brushing
- 1 tablespoon (15 g) harissa paste
- 3 large cloves garlic, grated or pressed
- 1½ teaspoons ground coriander

- 1 teaspoon ground cumin
- teaspoon fine sea salt
- ¼ teaspoon ground cinnamon
- ¼ teaspoon ground allspice
- ¼ teaspoon ground nutmeg
- 2 tablespoons (15 g) whole wheat pastry flour or (16 g) all-purpose flour
- 2 tablespoons (30 ml) fresh lemon juice, optional
- Olive oil, for brushing

Instructions

1. **To make the cuttings**: 20 cups Cover a small roll of muffins with 24 cups of spray oil.

2. Grate beans or peas in a large bowl: if there are only a few beans left, that's fine. Chop the top into small pieces (do not crush). Add onions, parsley, oil. Cover the harissa paste, garlic, coriander, cumin, salt, cinnamon, spice flour, nutmeg, and flour.

3. Stir to combine. If the mixture is dry and does not come together, add the lemon juice and stir to combine. Place a tablespoon of the round and round mixture (approximately 25 grams) on a ball and place it in a muffin pan. Repeat with the remaining bushes. Cover with a loose plastic wrap and refrigerate for 1 hour.

4. Heat the oven to 350 degrees F (180 degrees Celsius or gas mark 4).

5. Gently brush each bush with oil. Bake for 15 minutes, turn gently (fins will be brittle) and brush lightly with oil again. Bake for another 10 minutes or until golden brown.

6. Leave it on the muffin hook for 10 minutes before serving, as the soles of the foot will be brittle just outside the stove. Serve with drunken almonds. The buttercups are also delicious.

7. **For dehydration**: combine all ingredients in a food processor to combine. Occasionally, stop jamming the sides with a rubber spatula. Cover and keep for at least 1 hour in the refrigerator until ready to serve. Remnants can be stored in a refrigerated container for up to 3 days. The sink thickens after more than 24 hours after freezing. Use it, as it spreads on bread or adds more lemon juice to taste.

EASY SEITAN FOR TWO

Yield: 2 servings

Protein content per serving: 43 g

Ingredients

- ½ teaspoon freshly ground black pepper
- Pinch of fine sea salt
- 2 (each 4 ounces, or 113 g) Kind-to- Cows Seitan cutlets
- 1/3 cup (80 ml) vegetable broth
- 1 tablespoon (16 g) tomato paste
- 1 teaspoon balsamic vinegar

- 1 teaspoon Dijon mustard
- 1 teaspoon white miso
- 1 tablespoon (15 ml) high heat neutral-flavored oil
- 2 tablespoons (20 g) minced shallot

Instructions

1. Rub the pepper and salt evenly into the seitan cutlets.
2. Whisk together the broth, tomato paste, vinegar, mustard, and miso in a small bowl.
3. Heat the oil over medium-high heat in a large skillet.
4. Put the cutlets into the skillet and cook for 3 to 5 minutes, until browned. Turnover and cook the second side for 3 to 4 minutes until also browned. Remove the cutlets and set aside.
5. Reduce the heat to medium-low. Add the shallots. Cook and stir for 2 to 3 minutes, until softened. Be careful not to burn them. Scrape up any bits stuck to the skillet. Pour the broth mixture into the skillet. Bring to a simmer and stir for 3 to 4 minutes. Put the cutlets back into the skillet and turn to coat. Simmer for 3 to 4 minutes to heat the cutlets throughout. Spoon the sauce over the cutlets to serve.

PECAN-CRUSTED SEITAN CUTLETS WITH BRUSSELS SPROUTS

Yield: 2 servings

Protein content per serving: 51 g

Ingredients

For the cutlets:

- ½ cup (120 ml) unsweetened plain vegan milk
- 3 tablespoons (42 g) vegan mayonnaise
- 1 tablespoon (15 g) Dijon mustard
- ¼ teaspoon fine sea salt, plus a pinch
- ½ teaspoon ground black pepper, plus a pinch
- ½ cup plus 2 tablespoons (63 g) pecan halves, ground
- 3 tablespoons (15 g) panko crumbs

- ¼ teaspoons onion powder
- 2 (each 4 ounces, or 113 g) Kind-to* Cows Seitan cutlets
- High heat neutral-flavored oil, for cooking

For the brussels sprouts:

- 1 tablespoon (15 ml) olive oil
- 12 ounces (340 g) of well- sliced Brussels sprouts
- 2 tablespoons (30 ml) vegetable broth
- 1 teaspoon Dijon mustard
- 3 tablespoons (21 g) grated carrots
- Salt and pepper

Instructions

1. To make the cutlets: Whisk together the milk, mayonnaise, mustard, and a pinch each of salt and pepper in a shallow bowl. Combine the pecans, panko. Onion powder, and remaining salt and pepper on a plate. Stir to combine. Line a baking sheet with parchment paper. Using one "wet" hand and one "dry" hand, dip each cutlet in the milk mixture, then in the pecan mixture, turning to coat thoroughly. Put on the lined baking sheet and repeat with the second cutlet. Refrigerate for 15 minutes or up to 8 hours. This helps to set the coating so it will not fall off during cooking.

2. To cook the cutlets, heat a thin layer of oil in a large heavy-bottomed skillet. Cook the cutlets for 5 to 7 minutes until browned. Turnover and cook the second side for 4 to 6 minutes until also browned.

3. To make the Brussels sprouts: Heat the oil in a large skillet over medium-high heat. Add the Brussels sprouts. Cook for 6 to 8 minutes, stirring occasionally. The Brussels sprouts should have some dark spots and be tender. Whisk together the broth and mustard in a small bowl. Turn the heat off. But leave the skillet on the weather. Stir in the broth mixture and the carrots. The liquid should evaporate or be absorbed — season to taste with salt and pepper.

4. To serve, divide the Brussels sprouts between two plates and top each with a cutlet.

QUIT-THE-CLUCK SEITAN

Yield: 6 cutlets (4 ounces, or 113 g each)

Protein content per cutlet: 41 g

For the seitan:

- 1¼ cups (150 g) vital wheat gluten
- ¼ cup (30 g) chickpea flour
- 3 tablespoons (22 g) nutritional yeast
- 1 tablespoon (7 g) onion powder
- 2 teaspoons dried poultry seasoning
- 1 teaspoon garlic powder
- ½ teaspoon ground white pepper
- ¼ cup (180 ml) vegetable broth

- 2 teaspoons no chicken bouillon paste
- 1 tablespoon (15 ml) olive oil

1 tablespoon high heat neutral-flavored oil, for cooking

For the cooking broth:

- 2 cups (470 ml) vegetable broth
- 1 tablespoon (8 g) nutritional yeast
- 2 teaspoons dried poultry seasoning
- 2 teaspoons onion powder
- 1 teaspoon Dijon mustard Salt and pepper

Instructions

To make the seitan:

1. Preheat the oven to 300°F (150*C, or gas mark 2).
2. Stir the dry ingredients together in a medium-size bowl. Stir the wet ingredients together in a measuring cup.
3. Pour the wet ingredients into the dry ingredients and stir to combine. Knead with your hands until it forms a cohesive ball.
4. Add tablespoon vital wheat gluten (9 g) or broth (15 ml), if needed, to reach the desired consistency. Divide into 6 equal portions.
5. Sandwich a portion of dough between two pieces of parchment paper.

6. Roll each portion into a cutlet that is no more than 1/2 inch (1.3 cm) thick.

7. Heat the oil in a large skillet over medium-high heat. Cook the cutlets (in batches) for 3 to 5 minutes until browned.

8. Turnover and cook the second side for 3 minutes until browned.

9. To prepare the cooking broth:

10. Stir all the ingredients together in a 9 x 13 inch (22 x 23 cm) baking dish.

11. Put the cutlets in the broth and cover the pan tightly with foil. Bake for 1 hour.

12. Turn off the oven and let the seitan sit in the oven for 1 hour.

13. Cool the seitan in the broth. Store the seitan and the broth separately in airtight containers in the refrigerator for up to 3 days or freeze for up to two months.

BEST BAKED TOFU AND KALE

Yield: 4 servings

Protein content per serving: 19 g

Ingredients

- ¼ cup (30 g) whole wheat pastry flour or (31 g) all-purpose flour
- ½ teaspoon ground white pepper
- 1 recipe Best Baked Tofu prepared
- 2 tablespoons (30 ml) high heat neutral-flavored oil
- 3 cloves garlic, thinly sliced
- ¼ cup (40 g) minced shallot

- 2 tablespoons (7 g) minced sun-dried tomatoes
- 4 cups (268 g) kale, chopped
- 1 can (14.5 ounces, or 411 g) diced tomatoes
- ½ cup (120 ml) vegetable broth
- ½ cup (60 ml) dry white wine
- 2 tablespoons (5 g) chopped fresh basil
- Juice from ½ lemon
- Salt and pepper

Instructions

1. Preheat the oven to 350°F (180°C. or gas mark 4). Combine the flour and pepper on a plate. Coat the baked tofu slices with the mixture.

2. Heat the oil in a large skillet over medium-high heat.

3. Cook the tofu slices (in batches) for 3 to 4 minutes until browned. Turn over to cook the second side for 3 to 4 minutes until also browned. Put the tofu in the oven to keep warm.

4. In the same skillet, cook the garlic, shallot, and a pinch of salt over medium heat for 3 to 4 minutes, until fragrant. Add the sun-dried tomatoes, kale, tomatoes, broth, and wine (if using). Bring to a simmer, and then cook for 12 to 15 minutes until the kale is tender. Stir in the basil and lemon juice and season to taste with salt and pepper. Serve the tofu slices on top of the greens.

BROCCOLI & WALNUT PESTO

Yield: 4 servings

Ingredients

For the pesto:

- 1 head broccoli, cut into florets
- 75 g walnut pieces
- 2 cloves garlic
- juice of 1 lemon
- 2 tbsp. olive oil
- For the Pasta Alia Genovese:

- 500 g pasta
- 1 large floury potato, peeled and sliced fairly thinly
- 200 g fine green beans

Instructions

1. Boil a large pot of water, then add the broccoli and cook for 5-6 minutes. Remove with a slotted spoon and place in the blender.

2. Add the pasta and potato slices to the pot and boil again. Cook for 8 minutes, then add the green beans and cook for another 2 minutes or until the pasta is cooked.

3. (Potato slices break while cooking, don't panic, imagine!).

4. Meanwhile, add nuts, garlic, lemon and olive oil to the mixture with broccoli and cabbage to mix. Season generously with salt and pepper, then add a little water, cut again and continue cooking until it reaches a consistency similar to the sauce.

5. Drain the pasta, potatoes, and beans, then return to the pot and stir through the broccoli plague. Heat the oven over low heat and stir to remove the pest.

6. Serve immediately!

BROCCOLI, KALE, CHILI & HAZELNUT PIZZA'

Yield: 2 large pizzas

Ingredients

- 500 g Whole Meal Bread Mix
- 200 ml Passata with Garlic
- 1 red onion, peeled and finely sliced
- 6 sun-dried tomatoes, roughly chopped
- 75 g fresh curly kale, woody stalks removed and leaves roughly chopped
- 6-8 stalks purple sprouting broccoli, the lower half of

stalks removed

- 1 red chili, finely sliced
- handful hazelnuts, roughly chopped
- dried oregano
- black pepper
- extra virgin olive oil

Instructions

1. Pack the bread mix according to the instructions. Kneel and let it grow in a warm place for 45.45 minutes.

2. Meanwhile, prepare the meatballs and heat the oven to 200 degrees Celsius at 400 degrees C with protein content per serving of 6 gasoline and put it in the oven if using a pizza stone. (Check if your stove has a specific pizza setting, many do, and that makes a big difference).

3. Spread the dough on a floured surface and divide it in two. Insert each section into a ground ball and then roll with a roller in a 30 cm circle.

4. When all the tanks are ready, and the stove is at maximum temperature, remove the pizza from the oven (or grease a baking sheet) or place the dough on the stone surface. Protein on each plate, cover with half the pasta, then the onion. Sprinkle with cabbage, broccoli, peppers, and hazelnuts, then sprinkle with

mint and black pepper and sprinkle with olive oil. Repeat for the second pizza.

5. Bake for 8-10 minutes until the slices brown and the base is well cooked.

GRÖNSAKSBULLAR (SWEDISH VEGAN MEATBALLS)

frying)

- 1 tsp ready-chopped garlic Protein content per serving garlic puree
- 2 carrots
- 1 red pepper
- large handful curly kale
- 400 g tin chickpeas
- 2 tbsp. olive oil
- 2 tbsp. nutritional yeast flakes (optional)
- 1 tsp vegetable stock powder
- 2 tbsp. gram flour

- a little plain flour for dusting
- **For the sauce:**
- 1 tbsp. dairy-free margarine
- 1 tbsp. plain flour
- 200 ml dairy-free milk (soy, nut or oat)
- 125 ml of boiling water
- 1 tsp vegetable stock powder
- 125 ml dairy-free cream (soy or oat)
- 2 tsp wholegrain mustard
- soy sauce

Instructions

1. Cook the peas in the microwave or a small pot for 2 minutes. Drain and set aside to cool.
2. Peel the onion and cut it into quarters, then use a mini crusher or a food chopper (or cut it by hand).
3. Heat the oil in a large pot or large saucepan with oil and add the onions and garlic. Cook over medium heat.
4. Peel the carrots and cut them into approximately 4-5 slices, then finely chop the crushed protein content in each food processor and add it to the onions. Then, chop the peppers in the same way, then cook the peas and the curried cabbage. Let all the vegetables cook over medium heat.

5. Drain and wash the chickpeas, then sprinkle with olive oil in a mini crusher or food processor in a nonstick skillet. Add to the pot, then sprinkle the yeast slices, the powdered broth, the warm flour, and a generous salt and pepper sauce. Mix all the ingredients, then remove from heat and let cool enough to cook.

6. Sprinkle a handful of crushers and flour with a little flour, then glue a teaspoon of the mixture, wrap it tightly in a ball in your hand and place it on a crushing board. Repeat until the entire combination is used; It should have approximately 20 types of meat.

7. Cover the bottom of a large pot with rapeseed or sunflower oil and fry the meatballs and turn until golden brown. Pour the cup into a plate covered with paper towels to drain the excess oil.

8. To make the sauce, heat the margarine in a small saucepan, stir the flour, and cook over medium heat for 2 minutes. Add non-dairy milk, water, powdered cream, and non-dairy cream and stir to mix until a thick and shiny sauce consistency is achieved. Add the mustard and stir, then add a few drops of soy sauce at a time and try everything you want so that the condiments do not reach the right level.

9. Serve the meatballs with the sauce on top, with mashed potatoes or French fries.

CHIPOTLE BLACK BEAN CHILI WITH NACHOS

Yield: 2 servings

Ingredients

- 2 tbsp. rapeseed or sunflower oil
- 1 red onion
- 1 carrot
- handful fresh coriander
- 1 tsp ready-chopped garlic Protein content per serving garlic puree
- 2-3 tsp chipotle paste (to your taste - 3 tsp is fairly spicy)
- 1 red pepper
- 400 g tin black beans
- 400 g tin chopped tomatoes
- pinch sugar
- salt and black pepper

Instructions

1. Heat the oil in a large pot or a large bowl with oil. Peel the onions and carrots and remove the coriander stems from the leaves (remove them later).

2. To chop onions, carrots, and coriander, use a mini crusher or food and then add it to the pot.

3. Add garlic and pea paste to the pot and stir. Chop the seeds and finely chop the peppers and add them to the pan.

4. Drain and wash the black beans and add them to the pot.

5. Chop the tomatoes and sugar, then season with salt and black pepper. Then cover it with a lid and heat it over high heat. Cook for 8-10 minutes, stirring constantly. Adjust and adjust seasoning if necessary.

6. Chop the coriander leaves thoroughly and chop the peppers before serving with rice, fajita or a handful of French fries.

7. Heat the oil in a large pan. Half or a quarter of each giant mushroom and drop the smaller ones entirely and add them to the pot. Chop and chop the scallions and add to the pot with peanut nuts.

8. Fill a pot with boiling water and add the noodles. Simmer for 5-6 minutes until freshly cooked. Drain and reserve.

9. In a glass or small bowl, mix the pepper sauce, soy sauce, and water with the smooth saucer.

10. When the mushrooms are cooked, and the peanuts are golden brown, pour the sauce into the pan and

add the noodles when bubbling. Stir to combine, then serve immediately.

EXOTIC MUSHROOM & CASHEW SWEET CHILI NOODLES

Yield: 2 Servings

Ingredients

- 2 tbsp. rapeseed or sunflower oil
- 200 g mixed 'exotic' mushrooms
- 4 spring onions
- 3 tbsp. cashew nuts
- 150 g (3 nests) whole-wheat noodles
- 3 tbsp. sweet chili sauce
- 2 tbsp. soy sauce
- 150 ml water

Instructions

1. Heat the oil in a large pot or a large pan with oil. Peel the onions and carrots and remove the coriander stems from the leaves (remove them later). To chop onions, carrots, and coriander, use a mini crusher or food and then add it to the pot.
2. Add garlic and pea paste to the pot and stir. Chop the seeds and finely chop the peppers and add them to the pan.

3. Drain and wash the black beans and add them to the pot. Chop the tomatoes and sugar, then season with salt and black pepper. Then cover it with a lid and heat it over high heat. Cook for 8-10 minutes, stirring constantly. Adjust and adjust seasoning if necessary.

4. Chop the coriander leaves thoroughly and chop the peppers before serving with rice, fajita or a handful of French fries.

SEED AND NUT ICE CREAM

Yield: 1 quart (950 ml), or 8 servings

Protein content per serving: 9 g

Ingredients

For the nuts:

- 1 1/3 tablespoons (30 g) pure maple syrup
- 1/3 teaspoon ground cinnamon
- ¼ teaspoon ground nutmeg
- ¼ teaspoon fine sea salt
- 1/3 cup (50 g) walnut or pecan halves

For the ice cream:

- 1/3 cup (128 g) tahini
- ⅓ cup (128 g) natural creamy cashew butter or peanut butter
- 12 ounces (340 g) soft silken tofu, or ugly or vanilla vegan yogurt
- 1/3 cup plus 2 tablespoons (200 g) agave nectar
- ¼ cup (60 ml) full-fat coconut milk
- 1/3 teaspoon ginger powder
- 1/3 teaspoon ground cinnamon
- 1½ teaspoons pure vanilla extract

Instructions

1. **To make the nuts:** Preheat the oven to 325°F (170°C, or gas mark 3).

2. In a medium bowl, mix maple syrup, cinnamon, nutmeg, and salt. Add half of the nut or walnut and stir to foam. Place on a baking sheet with oil on a nonstick baking sheet and bake for 8 minutes. Stir for another 4 to 6 minutes to heat and dry and be careful not to dry. Before crushing, remove from oven and allow to cool completely. Set aside.

3. **To make ice cream**: Freeze your ice cream tub for at least 24 hours.

4. Put all the ingredients in the blender and mix until smooth. Try a little of the mixture to make sure it is sweet and sweet enough to your liking and, if desired, add 1 tablespoon (15 ml) at a time to the sweetener. If you make adjustments, mix again.

5. Transfer the mixture to the ice cream machine and follow the ice cream preparation instructions. Add chopped nuts during the last 5 minutes of shake. Transfer to a container and refrigerate for 2 hours. After more than a couple of hours, the ice cream does not want to be poured directly from the freezer, so let it sit for 15 minutes at room temperature.

PROVENTALE TOFU SALAD SANDWICHES

Yield: 6 to 9 sandwiches. 3 cups (540 g) tofu salad

Protein content per sandwich (with salad): 5 Q

Ingredients

- 1¼ teaspoons neutral-flavored oil
- 1 pound (454 g) super firm tofu, cut into ½-inch (6 mm) cubes
- 1¼ teaspoons vegan Worcestershire sauce
- ¼ cup (112 g) vegan mayonnaise
- 3 tablespoons (30 g) minced red onion
- ½ cup (30 g) coarsely chopped toasted walnuts
- 3 tablespoons (11 g) minced fresh parsley
- 2 tablespoons (13 g) minced pitted kalamata olives
- 1 tablespoon (4 g) minced soft or oil-packed (rinsed and patted dry) sun-dried tomatoes
- 1 tablespoon (15 ml) white balsamic vinegar
- 1 tablespoon (15 ml) fresh lemon juice
- 2 teaspoons minced capers
- 1 large or 2 small cloves of garlic, grated or pressed
- ¼ teaspoon herbes de Provence or dried basil
- ¼ teaspoon red pepper flakes

- White or black ground pepper
- Salt
- 12 to 18 slices of vegan sourdough
- bread or favorite vegan bread, toasted
- Favorite vegan pesto, as needed

Instructions

1. Place the oil in a large skillet and heat on medium-high heat. Add the tofu and saute until lightly browned, often stirring, for about 6 minutes. Add the Worcestershire sauce and stir to combine, sauteing another 2 minutes. Remove from the heat to let cool.

2. In a large bowl, combine the mayonnaise, onion, walnuts, parsley, olives, sun-dried tomatoes, vinegar, lemon juice, capers, garlic, herbes de Provence, red pepper flakes, and pepper. Stir the cooled tofu into the mayonnaise mixture. Adjust the seasonings if needed. Cover and place in the refrigerator for at least 3 hours, or overnight, to let the flavors blend.

3. Spread a thin layer of pesto on all bread slices. Place ½ cup (60 g) of tofu salad evenly on a slice of bread or as much as will fit on the slice. Be careful not to be too generous, so that the tofu cubes don't fall out as you eat. Cover with a second slice of bread. Repeat until you run out of ingredients. The Yield will vary depending on the size of the sliced bread.

4. Leftovers of the salad can be stored in an airtight container in the refrigerator for up to 4 days.

CASSOULET

Yield: 8 to 10 servings

Protein Content Per Serving: 22 g

- Ingredients
- ¼ cup (60 ml) olive oil, divided
- 4 ounces (113 g) Quit-the-Cluck Seitan, chopped
- 1/3 of a Smoky Sausage, chopped
- 1½ cups (240 g) chopped onion
- 2 ounces (57 g) minced shiitake mushrooms
- 2 large carrots, peeled, sliced into ¼-inch (6 mm) rounds
- 2 stalks celery, chopped
- 1½ cups (355 ml) vegetable broth, divided
- 1 teaspoon liquid smoke
- 3 cans (each 15 ounces, or 425 g) white beans of choice, drained and rinsed
- 1 can (14.5 ounces, or 410 g) diced tomatoes, undrained
- 2 tablespoons (32 g) tomato paste 1 tablespoon (15 ml) tamari
- 1 tablespoon (18 g) no chicken bouillon paste, or 2 bouillon cubes, crumbled
- 2 tablespoons (8 g) minced fresh parsley

- 2 teaspoons dried thyme
- ½ teaspoon dried rosemary Salt and pepper
- 2 cups (200 g) fresh bread crumbs
- ½ cup (40 g) panko crumbs

Instructions

1. Preheat the oven to 375°F (190°C, or gas mark 5).
2. Heat 1 tablespoon (15 ml) of olive oil in a large skillet over medium heat.
3. Add the seitan and sausage. Cook for 4 to 6 minutes, occasionally stirring, until browned. Transfer to a plate and set aside.
4. Add the onion and a pinch of salt to the same skillet. Cook for 5 to 7 minutes until translucent. Transfer to the same plate. Add the shiitakes, carrots, and celery to the skillet and cook for 2 minutes. Add 1 tablespoon (15 ml) vegetable broth and the liquid smoke. Cook for 2 to 3 minutes, stirring until the liquid is absorbed or evaporated.
5. Return the seitan and onions to the skillet and add the beans, tomatoes, tomato paste, tamari, bouillon, parsley, thyme, rosemary, and remaining broth. Cook for 3 to 4 minutes, stirring to combine. Season with salt and pepper to taste and transfer to a large casserole pan.

6. Toss together the fresh bread crumbs, panko crumbs, and the remaining 3 tablespoons (45 ml) olive oil in a small bowl. Spread evenly over the bean mixture. Bake for 30 to 35 minutes until the crumbs are browned.

DOUBLE-GARLIC BEAN AND VEGETABLE SOUP

Yield: 4 servings

Protein content per serving: 21 g

Ingredients

- 1 tablespoon (15 ml) olive oil
- 1 teaspoon fine sea salt
- 1 (240 g) minced onion 5 cloves garlic, minced
- 2 cups (220 g) chopped red potatoes
- ⅔ cup (96 g) sliced carrots
- Protein content per serving cup (60 g) chopped celery
- 1 teaspoon Italian seasoning blend
- Protein content per serving teaspoon red pepper flakes, or to taste
- Protein content per serving teaspoon celery seed
- 4 cups water (940 ml), divided
- 1 can (14.5 ounces, or 410 g) crushed tomatoes or tomato puree
- 1 head roasted garlic
- 2 tablespoons (30 g) prepared vegan pesto, plus more for garnish
- 2 cans (each 15 ounces, or 425 g) different kinds of

white beans, drained and rinsed

- Protein content per serving cup (50 g)
- 1-inch (2.5 cm) pieces green beans
- Salt and pepper

Instructions

1. Heat the oil and salt in a large soup pot over medium heat. Add the onion, garlic, potatoes, carrots, and celery. Cook for 4 to 6 minutes, occasionally stirring, until the onions are translucent. Add the seasoning blend, red pepper flakes, and celery seed and stir for 2 minutes. Add 3 cups (705 ml) of the water and the crushed tomatoes.

2. Combine the remaining 1 cup (235 ml) water and the roasted garlic in a blender. Process until smooth. Add to the soup mixture and bring to a boil. Reduce the heat to simmer and cook for 30 minutes.

3. Stir in the pesto, beans, and green beans. Simmer for 15 minutes. Taste and adjust the seasonings. Serve each bowl with a dollop of pesto, if desired.

HUMMUS BISQUE

Yield: 4 servings

Protein content per serving: 14 g

Ingredients

- 1 tablespoon (15 ml) toasted sesame oil ¼ cup (40 g) chopped shallot
- 2 teaspoons grated or pressed garlic 1 teaspoon ground cumin
- 1 teaspoon sambal oelek or harissa paste, or to taste
- ⅓ teaspoon smoked paprika
- 2 cups (328 g) cooked chickpeas ½ cup (80 ml) fresh lemon juice
- 3 cups (705 ml) vegetable broth, more if needed
- ⅓ cup (128 g) tahini
- Salt and white pepper
- ¼ cup (4 g) chopped fresh cilantro or (15 g) parsley (or a combination of the two), for garnish
- Toasted cumin seeds, for garnish, optional
  Lemon zest, for garnish, optional

Instructions

1. Heat the oil in a large pot. Add the shallot, garlic, cumin, sambal oelek or harissa paste, paprika, and chickpeas. Cook on medium heat, stirring often until the shallot is tender and the preparation is fragrant about 4 minutes. Add the lemon juice, stirring to combine.

2. Add the broth and bring to a boil. Lower the heat, cover with a lid, and simmer for 10 minutes. Add the tahini, stirring to combine. Note that the tahini might look curdled when you add it, but it will be okay after simmerging and blending. Cover with the lid and simmer for another 5 minutes.

3. Use a handheld blender and blend the mixture until smooth. Be careful: The liquid will be hot, so watch for spatters! You can also use a regular blender to puree the soup, be careful while transferring the hot liquid. If you find the bisque a little thick for your taste once blended, add extra broth as needed.

4. Adjust the seasonings to taste and serve garnished with cilantro, parsley, cumin seeds, and lemon zest.

5. Lettovers can be slowly reheated by simmering in a small saucepan for about 6 minutes until heated through. Stir occasionally while reheating and be careful not to scorch what is a rather thick soup.

MEAN BEAN MINESTRONE

Yield: 8 to 10 servings

Protein content per serving: 9g

Ingredients

- 1 tablespoon (15 ml) olive oil
- 1/3 cup (80 g) chopped red onion
- 4 cloves garlic, grated or pressed
- 1 leek, white and light green parts, trimmed and chopped (about 4 ounces, or 113 g)
- 2 carrots, peeled and minced (about 4 ounces, or 113 g)
- 2 ribs of celery, minced (about 2 ounces, or 57 g)
- 2 yellow squashes, trimmed and chopped (about 8 ounces, or 227 g)
- 1 green bell pepper, trimmed and chopped (about 8 ounces, or 227 g)
- 1 tablespoon (16 g) tomato paste
- 1 teaspoon dried oregano
- 1 teaspoon dried basil
- ⅓ teaspoon smoked paprika
- '¼ to ¼ teaspoon cayenne pepper, or to taste
- 2 cans (each 15 ounces, or 425 g) diced fire-roasted tomatoes

- 4 cups (940 ml) vegetable broth, more if needed
- 3 cups (532 g) cannellini beans, or other white beans
- 2 cups (330 g) cooked farro, or other whole grain or pasta
- Salt, to taste
- Nut and Seed Sprinkles, for garnish, optional and to taste

Instructions

1. In a large pot, add the oil, onion, garlic, leek, carrots, celery, yellow squash, bell pepper, tomato paste, oregano, basil, paprika, and cayenne pepper. Cook on medium-high heat, stirring often until the vegetables start to get tender, about 6 minutes.
2. Add the tomatoes and broth. Bring to a boil, lower the heat, cover with a lid, and simmer 15 minutes.
3. Add the beans and simmer another 10 minutes. Add the farro and simmer 5 more minutes to heat the farro.
4. Note that this is a thick minestrone. If there are leftovers (which taste even better, by the way), the soup will thicken more once chilled.
5. Add extra broth if you prefer a thinner soup and adjust seasoning if needed. Add Nut and Seed Sprinkles on each portion upon serving, if desired.

6. Store leftovers in an airtight container in the refrigerator for up to 5 days. The minestrone can also be frozen for up to 3 months.

SUSHI RICE AND BEAN STEW

Yield: 4 to 6 servings

Protein content per serving: 11 g

Ingredients

For the sushi rice:

- 1 cup (208 g) dry sushi rice, thoroughly rinsed until water runs clear and drained
- 1¾ cups (295 ml) water
- 1 tablespoon (15 ml) fresh lemon juice
- 1 teaspoon toasted sesame oil
- 1 teaspoon sriracha
- 1 teaspoon tamari
- 1 teaspoon agave nectar or brown rice syrup

For the stew:

- 1 tablespoon (15 ml) toasted sesame oil
- 9 ounces (255 g) minced carrot (about 4 medium carrots)
- 1/3 cup (80 g) chopped red onion or ¼ cup (40 g) minced shallot
- 2 teaspoons grated fresh ginger or ⅓ teaspoon ginger powder
- 4 cloves garlic, grated or pressed

- I½ cups (246 g) cooked chickpeas

- 1 cup (155 g) frozen, shelled edamame

- 3 tablespoons (45 ml) seasoned rice vinegar

- 2 tablespoons (30 ml) tamari

- 2 teaspoons sriracha, or to taste

- 1 cup (235 ml) mushroom-soaking broth

- 2 cups (470 ml) vegetable broth

- 2 tablespoons (36 g) white miso

- 2 tablespoons (16 g) toasted white sesame seeds

Instructions

1. **To make the sushi rice:** Combine the rice and water in a rice cooker, cover with the lid, and cook until the water is absorbed without lifting the lid. (Alternatively, cook the rice on the stove top, following the directions on the package.)

2. While the rice is cooking, combine the remaining sushi rice ingredients in a large bowl.

3. Let the rice steam for 10 minutes in the rice cooker with the lid still on. Gently fold the cooked rice into the dressing. Set aside.

4. **To make the stew:** Heat the oil in a large pot on medium-high heat. Add the carrots, onion, ginger, and garlic. Lower the temperature to medium and cook until the vegetables start to get tender, stirring often about 4 minutes.

5. Add the chickpeas, edamame, vinegar, tamari, and sriracha. Stir and cook for another 4 minutes. Add the broths, and bring back to a slow boil. Cover with a lid, lower the heat, and simmer for 10 minutes.

6. Place the miso in a small bowl and remove 3 tablespoons (45 ml) of the broth from the pot. Stir into the miso to thoroughly combine. Stir the miso mixture back into the pan, and remove from the heat.

7. Divide the rice among 4 to 6 bowls, depending on your appetite. Add approximately 1 cup (235 ml) of the stew on top of each portion of rice. Add 1 teaspoon of sesame seeds on top of each serving, and serve immediately.

8. If you do not plan on eating this dish in one shot, keep the rice and stew separated and store in the refrigerator for up to 4 days.

9. When reheating the stew, do not bring to a boil. Slowly warm the rice with the stew on medium heat in a small saucepan until heated through.

GIARDINIERA CHILI

Yield: 8 servings

Protein content per serving: 28 g

Ingredients

- 1 tablespoon (15 ml) neutral-flavored oil
- 1 medium red onion, chopped
- 4 carrots, peeled and minced (9 ounces, or 250 g)
- 2 zucchini, trimmed and minced (11 ounces, or 320 g)
- 4 Roma tomatoes, diced (14 ounces, or 400 g)
- 4 cloves garlic, grated or pressed
- 1 tablespoon (8 g) mild to medium chili powder
- 1 teaspoon ground cumin
- ½ teaspoon smoked paprika
- ½ teaspoon liquid smoke
- ¼ teaspoon fine sea salt, or to taste
- ¼ teaspoon cayenne pepper, or to taste
- 2 tablespoons (32 g) tomato paste
- 1 can (15 ounces, or 425 g) diced fire-roasted tomatoes
- ½ cup (120 ml) vegetable broth
- ½ cup (120 ml) mushroom-soaking broth or extra vegetable broth
- 1 can (15 ounces, or 425 g) pinto beans, drained and

rinsed

- 1 can (15 ounces, or 425 g) black beans, drained and rinsed
- ½ cup (60 g) nutritional yeast

Instructions

1. Heat the oil on medium-high in a large pot and add the onion, carrots, zucchini, tomatoes, and garlic. Cook for 6 minutes, stirring occasionally until the carrots start to get tender. Add the chili powder, cumin, paprika, liquid smoke, salt, cayenne pepper, and tomato paste, stirring to combine. Cook another 2 minutes. Add the diced tomatoes, broths, beans, and nutritional yeast. Bring to a low boil. Lower the heat, cover with a lid, and simmer 15 minutes, stirring occasionally. Remove the lid and simmer for another 5 minutes.
2. Serve on top of a cooked whole grain of choice or with your favorite chili accompaniments.
3. Leftovers can be stored in an airtight container in the refrigerator for up to 4 days or frozen for up to 3 months.

SHORBA (LENTIL SOUP)

Yield: 4 to 6 servings

Protein content per serving: 10 g

Ingredients

- 1 tablespoon (15 ml) olive oil
- 1 medium onion, minced
- 1 large carrot, peeled and chopped
- 1 fist-size russet potato, cut into small cubes (about 7 ounces, or 198 g)
- 4 large cloves garlic, minced
- 2 teaspoons grated fresh ginger root
- 1 to 2 teaspoons berbere, to taste
- 1/3 teaspoon turmeric
- 1 cup (192 g) brown lentils, picked over and rinsed
- 6 cups (1.4 L) water, more if desired
- 1 tablespoon (16 g) tomato paste
- 1 tablespoon (18 g) vegetable bouillon paste, or 2 bouillon cubes
- Salt and pepper

Instructions

1. Heat the oil in a large soup pot over medium heat. Add the onion, carrot, and potato. Cook for 5 to 7 minutes, stirring occasionally until the onions are translucent. Stir in the garlic, ginger, berbere, turmeric, and lentils and cook and stir for 1 minute until fragrant. Add the water, tomato paste, and bouillon. Bring to a boil, and then reduce the heat to a simmer. Cook for 30 minutes, stirring occasionally until the lentils are tender. Taste and adjust the seasonings.

SPLIT PEA PATTIES

Yield: 8 patties

Protein content per patty: 10 g

Ingredients

- ¾ cup (148 g) dry green split peas, cooked al dente (See Recipe Note.), drained
- 3 tablespoons (45 ml) fresh lemon juice 1 tablespoon (15 ml) neutral-flavored oil 3 cloves garlic, grated or pressed
- ⅓ cup (53 g) minced red onion
- ¼ cup (4 g) minced fresh cilantro or (15 g) fresh parsley
- 1 teaspoon ground cumin
- 1 teaspoon garam masala
- 1/3 teaspoon fine sea salt
- 1/3 teaspoon paprika (smoked or regular)
- ⅓ teaspoon turmeric
- '¼ teaspoon cayenne pepper
- ¼ cup (30 g) whole wheat pastry flour or (31 g) all-purpose flour
- 2 tablespoons (24 g) potato starch or (16 g) cornstarch
- 1/3 teaspoon baking powder

- Water, as needed
- Nonstick cooking spray or oil spray

Instructions

1. Place the cooked split peas in a food processor and pulse about 15 times to break down the peas slightly. You're not looking to puree them, but to make it so the mixture will hold together better to form patties. In a large bowl, combine the split peas with lemon juice, oil, garlic, onion, cilantro, cumin, garam masala, salt, paprika, turmeric, and cayenne pepper until thoroughly mixed. Add the flour, starch, and baking powder on top.

2. Stir until thoroughly mixed. If the mixture is dry and crumbly, stir water into it, 1 tablespoon (15 ml) at a time until the mixture holds together better. We usually have to add 2 tablespoons (30 ml) of water. Refrigerate for 1 hour.

3. Preheat the oven to 350°F (180°C, or gas mark 4).

4. Divide the mixture into 8 patties (each one a scant but packed '¼ cup, or 60 g) of a little under 3 inches (7 cm) in diameter and ^-inch (1.3 cm) in thickness. Place on a baking sheet lined with parchment paper or press into a lightly greased whoopie pie pan. Lightly coat the top with cooking spray.

5. Bake for 15 minutes on one side, flip, lightly coat with cooking spray, and bake for another 10 minutes until golden brown.

6. Store leftovers in an airtight container in the refrigerator for up to 4 days. Gently reheat in a pan or in the oven or enjoy cold or at room temperature.

SAVORY EDAMAME MINI CAKES

Yield: 14 to 16 cakes, plus ¼ cup (60 ml) sauce

Protein content per cake (with sauce): 3 g

Ingredients

For the sauce:

- 3 tablespoons (45 ml) tamari
- 1 teaspoon smooth peanut butter
- 1 teaspoon seasoned rice vinegar, or to taste
- 1 teaspoon sambal oelek, or to taste

For the cakes:

- 1 cup (150 g) frozen, shelled edamame, thawed
- ¼ cup (36 g) minced bell pepper (any color)
- 3 tablespoons (30 g) minced red onion
- 2 cloves garlic, minced
- 5-spice powder Generous
- ¼ teaspoon fine sea salt
- Pinch of ground black pepper
- 1 cup (140 g) whole spelt flour
- 1 ½ cup plus 1 tablespoon (95 ml) unsweetened plain vegan milk
- ⅔ cup (53 g) panko crumbs
- 2 tablespoons (16 g) toasted sesame seeds

- 2 tablespoons (30 ml) high-heat neutral-flavored oil

Instructions

1. **To make the sauce:** In a small bowl, whisk together the tamari, peanut butter, rice vinegar, and sambal oelek until smooth. Set aside.

2. **To make the cakes:** Put the edamame, bell pepper, onion, garlic, 5-spice powder, salt, and pepper in a medium-size bowl. Stir to combine. Stir in the flour, then the milk to form a dough. It should be shapeable, but some of the edamame may poke out. Combine the panko and the sesame seeds on a shallow plate.

3. Heat the oil in a large skillet over medium-high heat.

4. Scoop 1 tablespoon (26 g) of the mixture and shape it into a small round no more than '1/4 inch (1.3 cm) thick and about 1¼ inches (3.8 cm) in diameter. Put it in the panko mixture and pat to coat well on both sides, continuing to shape it into a small cake. Repeat until all the cakes have been formed. Put half of the cakes into the skillet and cook for 3 to 5 minutes until golden brown. Turn over to cook the second side for 2 to 4 minutes, until also golden brown. Drain on a paper towel-lined plate. Cook the remaining cakes in the same manner, adding more oil if needed serve with the sauce for dipping.

QUINOA EDAMAME ROLLS

Yield: 14 rolls, plus scant ⅔ cup (175 ml) dressing

Protein content per roll (with dressing): 4 g

Ingredients

For the dressing:

- 4 Protein content per serving tablespoons (68 ml) fresh lemon juice
- 1 Protein content per serving tablespoons (23 ml) toasted sesame oil
- 1 Protein content per serving tablespoons (23 ml) sriracha
- 1 Protein content per serving tablespoons (23 ml) tamari
- 1 Protein content per serving tablespoons (30 g) agave nectar or brown rice syrup
- 1 Protein content per serving tablespoons (12 g) toasted sesame seeds
- 1 large clove garlic, grated or pressed

For the rolls:

- ⅔ cup (116 g) cooked shelled edamame
- ⅔ cup (110 g) packed cooked and cooled quinoa
- Protein content per serving cup (45 g) packed minced

napa cabbage

- ¼ cup (27 g) toasted slivered almonds
- ¼ cup (20 g) chopped scallion
- 2 tablespoons (2 g) loosely packed chopped cilantro
- 2 tablespoons (24 g) packed peeled and grated daikon radish, liquid gently squeezed out before measuring
- 14 spring roll wrappers
- Nonstick cooking spray or oil spray

Instructions

1. **To make the dressing:** Combine all the ingredients in a small bowl, using a whisk. Set aside.

2. **To make the rolls:** Combine the edamame, quinoa, napa cabbage, almonds, scallion, cilantro, and daikon radish in a large bowl. Add '¼ cup (60 ml) of the dressing on top, stirring to combine. Set aside the rest of the dressing for serving.

3. Immerse the spring roll wrappers 1 sheet at a time in warm water to soften. Soak for a few seconds, until pliable. Handle carefully because the wraps tear easily. Drain on a clean kitchen towel before rolling.

4. To assemble, place 2 packed tablespoons (30 g) of filling per moistened wrapper.

5. Roll tightly and place on a plate. Repeat with remaining rolls. Be careful when separating the rolls:

The wraps might stick to one another a little, but won't tear if you separate them slowly.

6. Heat a large skillet on medium-high heat. Lower the heat to medium, lightly coat with cooking spray or oil spray, away from the heat. Place as many rolls as will fit in your skillet without overcrowding it, and cook the rolls on each side until light golden brown and crisp, about 4 minutes per side. Repeat with remaining rolls. Serve immediately with the remaining dressing.

7. Leftovers can be wrapped tightly and stored in the refrigerator for up to 3 days.

SPICY CHICKPEA FRIES

Yield: About 64 fries, or 4 servings

Protein content per serving: 14 g

Ingredients

- 4 cups (940 ml) vegetable broth
- 2 tablespoons (15 g) nutritional yeast
- 1 teaspoon fine sea salt
- 1 teaspoon onion powder
- 1 teaspoon garlic powder
- 1 teaspoon smoked paprika
- 1 teaspoon ground cumin
- 1 teaspoon ground coriander
- 1 teaspoon garam masala
- 2 cups (240 g) chickpea flour, sifted
- ¼ cup (30 g) cornflour, sifted (not cornstarch, preferably organic)
- Nonstick cooking spray
- Up to ¼ cup (60 ml) olive oil, for brushing

Instructions

1. Combine the broth, nutritional yeast, salt, onion powder, garlic powder, paprika, cumin, coriander, and garam masala in a large saucepan and bring to a boil. Lower the heat, and then (and this is important to avoid clumping) *slowly* stream in the flours, whisking constantly. Reduce the heat to medium-low, switch to stirring with a wooden spoon almost constantly, and cook for 6 minutes or until the mixture is so thick that when you slash a line through its center with the spoon all the way to the bottom of the pan, the line remains and the mixture doesn't slide back to cover the bottom of the pan. Be sure to adjust the temperature, if needed, to avoid scorching.

2. Remove from the heat. Spread evenly in an 8-inch (20 cm) square baking pan coated with cooking spray, using an angled spatula. Do not cover the pan. Once it's cool enough, place it in the refrigerator for at least 2 hours.

3. Remove the chilled mixture from the pan. Cut into 'Protein content per serving2-inch (1.3 cm) strips, flipping those strips on the side (they will be approximately 1-inch [2.5 cm] wide once flipped) and cutting them in two lengthwise again to obtain two 'Protein content per serving-inch (1.3 cm) wide, 8-

inch (20 cm) long strips. Then cut both strips once in the middle widthwise. You should get fries of approximately 4 x 'Protein content per serving inches (10 x 1.3 cm).

4. Preheat the oven to 425°F (220°C, or gas mark 7). Lightly grease a large rimmed baking sheet with olive oil.

5. Lightly brush the fries with oil and space them evenly on the prepared sheet.

6. Bake for 15 minutes, flip the fries and bake for another 15 minutes or until golden brown and crispy. Serve immediately.

BAKED FALAFEL

Yield: 32 falafels

Protein content per falafel: 2 g

Ingredients

- Nonstick cooking spray
- 3 cups (492 g) cooked chickpeas
- ¼ cup (60 ml) fresh lemon juice
- 3 cloves garlic, minced
- ⅓ cup (20 g) packed fresh parsley
- 1/3 cup (5 g) packed fresh cilantro
- ⅓ cup (53 g) minced red onion
- 2 tablespoons (32 g) tahini
- 1 tablespoon (15 ml) toasted sesame oil
- 1 ground cumin
- 1 Protein content per serving teaspoons ground coriander
- ¼ teaspoon cayenne pepper
- Scant Protein content per serving teaspoon fine sea salt, or to taste
- 3 tablespoons (23 g) whole wheat pastry flour or all-purpose flour
- Protein content per serving teaspoon baking soda

- 2 tablespoons (30 ml) olive oil

Instructions

1. Preheat the oven to 400°F (200°C, or gas mark 6). Lightly coat 32 cups out of two 24-cup mini muffin tins with cooking spray.

2. Place the chickpeas, lemon juice, garlic, parsley, and cilantro in a food processor.

3. Consider doing this in a couple of batches, depending on the size of your food processor. Pulse a few times, stopping to scrape the sides with a rubber spatula: You're looking for a somewhat smooth texture but not precisely a paste. The beans should be broken down, but it's okay if a few pieces remain as long as the mixture is cohesive.

4. Remove from the food processor and place in a large bowl. Add the onion, tahini, sesame oil, cumin, coriander, cayenne pepper, and salt. Stir to combine. Add the flour and baking soda on top and stir until thoroughly combined.

5. Gather 1 packed tablespoon (18 g) of mixture per falafel, gently shape into a ball and place in the mini muffin tin. Repeat with the remaining dough. Lightly brush the tops with olive oil.

6. Bake for 15 minutes, carefully flip each falafel, and lightly brush with oil. Bake for another 8 minutes or until golden brown.

7. Remove from the oven and let stand 5 minutes before serving.

PUDLA

Yield: 2 to 4 servings

Protein content per serving: 9 g

Ingredients

- ¾ cup (180 ml) unsweetened plain vegan milk, plus extra if needed
- 2 tablespoons (30 ml) fresh lemon juice
- 1 cup (120 g) chickpea flour
- ⅓ teaspoon baking soda
- ⅓ teaspoon ground cumin
- ⅓ teaspoon ground coriander
- ⅓ teaspoon garam masala
- '¼ to ¼ teaspoon cayenne pepper, or to taste
- ⅓ teaspoon fine sea salt, or to taste
- 2 tablespoons (30 ml) olive oil
- 2 tablespoons (15 g) nutritional yeast
- 1 tablespoon (16 g) tahini
- ⅓ cup (40 g) minced red onion
- ⅓ cup (4 g) fresh cilantro leaves (not packed)
- 2 cloves garlic, grated or pressed
- Nonstick cooking spray or oil spray

Instructions

1. Combine the milk and lemon juice in a medium bowl. Let stand for two minutes to let the milk curdle. This is your "buttermilk."

2. In the meantime, whisk together the flour, baking soda, cumin, coriander, garam masala, cayenne pepper, and salt in a large bowl.

3. Add the olive oil, nutritional yeast, tahini, red onion, cilantro, and garlic to the buttermilk.

4. Add the wet ingredients to dry thoroughly, but do not overdo it. Let stand for 10 minutes. The dough will thicken. If it is thick enough to be unmanageable, add the milk needed to dilute it in 3 cups (60 ml).

5. Heat a large skillet over medium heat. Reduce heat to medium. Cover the pan gently and away from the heat of the floor with a baking spray or oil spray. Add the dough (approximately 3.5 ounces or 100 grams), spread it in a circle of just over 5 inches (13 cm). Let cook for about 4 minutes until the center bubbles and is not too dry but not too wet. Lift the edges of the hole carefully to make sure it is light golden brown, which is another sign of being ready to turn.

6. Carefully fork with a spoon and cook for another 4 minutes or until golden brown on one side.

7. Before cooking, cover the rest of the dough in three batches. Serve immediately.

THE WHOLE ENCHILADA

Yield: 12 to 14 enchiladas

Protein content per enchilada: 6 g

Ingredients

For the sauce:

- 2 tablespoons (30 ml) olive oil 1/3 cup (80 g) chopped red onion 4 ounces (113 g) tomato paste

- 1 tablespoon (15 ml) adobo sauce

- 1 tablespoon (8 g) mild to medium chili powder

- 1 teaspoon ground cumin
- 3 cloves garlic, grated or pressed
- ⅓ teaspoon fine sea salt, or to taste
- 2 tablespoons (15 g) whole wheat pastry flour or (16 g) all-purpose flour
- 2 cups (470 ml) water

For the filling:

- 1 Protein content per serving teaspoons olive oil
- ⅓ cup (53 g) chopped red onion
- 1 sweet potato, trimmed and peeled, chopped (about 8.8 ounces, or 250 g)
- 1 yellow squash, trimmed and chopped (about 5.3 ounces, or 150 g)
- 2 cloves garlic, grated or pressed
- 1 tablespoon (8 g) nutritional yeast
- 1 smoked paprika
- ¼ teaspoon liquid smoke
- Pinch of fine sea salt, or to taste
- 1 (258 g) cooked black beans
- 3 tablespoons (45 ml) enchilada sauce
- 12 to 14 corn tortillas
- 1 recipe Creamy Cashew Sauce
- Chopped fresh cilantro, to taste Hot sauce, to taste

Instructions

1. **To make the sauce:** Heat the oil on medium heat in a large skillet. Add the onion and cook until fragrant while occasionally stirring, about 2 minutes. Add the tomato paste, adobo sauce, chili powder, cumin, garlic, and salt. Saute for 2 minutes, stirring frequently. Sprinkle the flour on top and cook 2 minutes, stirring frequently. Slowly whisk in the water and cook until slightly thickened, about 6 minutes, frequently whisking to prevent clumps. Remove from the heat and set aside.

2. To make the filling: Heat the oil in a large skillet on medium heat. Add the onion and sweet potato and cook 6 minutes or until the potato starts to get tender, stirring occasionally. Add the squash and garlic and cook for 4 minutes, stirring occasionally. Add the nutritional yeast, paprika, liquid smoke, and salt, stir to combine, and cook for another minute. Add the beans and enchilada sauce and stir to combine. Cover the pan and simmer until the vegetables are completely tender about 4 minutes. Add a little water if the plants stick to the skillet. Adjust the seasonings if needed.

3. Preheat the oven to 350°F (180°C, or gas mark 4).

4. Place the sauce in a large shallow bowl. If you aren't using pre-shaped, uncooked tortillas, follow the instructions in the Recipe Notes to soften the tortillas

so that they are easier to work with. Ladle about 1/3 cup (80 ml) of enchilada sauce on the bottom of a 9 x 13-inch (23 x 33 cm) baking dish. Dip each tortilla in the sauce to coat only lightly. Don't be too generous and gently scrape off the excess sauce with a spatula; otherwise, you will run out of sauce. Add a scant ¼ cup (about 45 g) of the filling in each tortilla. Fold the tortilla over the filling, rolling like a cigar. Place the enchiladas in the pan, seam side down. Make sure to squeeze them in tight so that there's room in the dish for all of them. Top evenly with the remaining enchilada sauce. Add the Creamy Cashew Sauce consistently on top.

5. Bake for 20 to 25 minutes or until the top is set, and the enchiladas are heated through. Garnish with cilantro and serve with hot sauce.

MUJADDARA

- 1 tablespoon (15 ml) olive oil or melted coconut oil
- 2 white onions, chopped (10 ounces, or 340 g)
- 1 leek, thoroughly cleaned and sliced thinly, white and light green parts (6 ounces, or 170g)
- Vegetable broth or water, as needed
- 4 cloves garlic, grated or pressed
- ⅓ teaspoon fine sea salt, or to taste
- ⅓ teaspoon ground cinnamon
- ⅓ teaspoon ground cumin
- ⅓ teaspoon ground coriander
- ⅓ teaspoon paprika
- ¼ teaspoon cayenne pepper, or to taste

- 2 tablespoons (12 g) chopped fresh mint
- 2 tablespoons (8 g) chopped fresh parsley or (2 g) cilantro
- Zest and juice of a small organic lemon
- ⅓ cup (35 g) chopped toasted peanuts, cashews, or pine nuts, optional

Instructions

1. Place the lentils and rice in a rice cooker. Cover with the broth, and stir to combine. Cover with the lid and cook until tender, 40 to 45 minutes. (Alternatively, cook the lentils and rice on the stovetop, following the directions on the package of rice.)

2. In a large skillet, add the oil and heat on medium heat. Add the onions and leek and saute until browned, about 15 minutes. Add vegetable broth, 1 tablespoon (15 ml) at a time, as needed, if the onions stick to the pan during that time. Add the garlic, salt, cinnamon, cumin, coriander, paprika, and cayenne pepper, stirring to combine. Stop stirring and cook until the onions are crisped and the spices toasted and fragrant, about 5 minutes.

3. Place the lentils and rice in a large bowl and add the spiced onions on top; thoroughly and gently fold the onions into the lentils and rice. Once you are ready to serve, fold the mint, parsley or cilantro, zest, and

lemon juice into the mujaddara, and garnish each serving with nuts. Adjust the seasonings as needed.

4. Leftovers can be stored in an airtight container in the refrigerator for up to 4 days. Note that this dish tastes even better when it gets to sit for a while. Gently reheat before serving.

BLACK BEAN AND AVOCADO SALAD

Yield: 4 servings

Protein content per serving: 8 g.

Ingredients

- 1 cup (172 g) cooked black beans
- ⅓ cup (82 g) frozen corn (run under hot water, drained)
- 3 tablespoons (15 g) minced scallion
- 6 cherry tomatoes, cut into quarters
- 2 cloves garlic, minced
- 1 teaspoon minced fresh cilantro, or to taste

- Pinch of dried oregano 1 chipotle in adobo
- 1 tablespoon (15 ml) fresh lemon juice
- 1 tablespoon (15 ml) apple cider vinegar 1 tablespoon (15 ml) vegetable broth
- 1 teaspoon nutritional yeast
- 2 tablespoons (15 g) roasted salted pepitas (hulled pumpkin seeds)
- 2 avocados, pitted, peeled, and chopped
- Salt and pepper

Instructions

1. Combine the beans, corn, scallion, cherry tomatoes, garlic, cilantro, and oregano in a medium-size bowl. Using a small blender or a mortar and pestle, thoroughly combine the chipotle, lemon juice, vinegar, broth, and nutritional yeast to form a dressing. Pour over the bean mixture and stir in the pepitas. Gently stir in the avocados. Season to taste with salt and pepper. Serve promptly so that the avocado doesn't discolor.

TABBOULEH VERDE

Yield: 4 to 6 servings

Protein content per serving: 9 g

Ingredients

- 1 cup (186 g) dry whole-wheat couscous
- ⅓ cup (120 ml) vegetable broth, brought to a boil
- 3 tablespoons (45 ml) extra-virgin olive oil
- 2 tablespoons (30 ml) fresh lemon juice
- 2 tablespoons (30 ml) fresh lime juice
- 1½ cups (258 g) cooked black beans
- 1½ cups (225 g) diced heirloom green tomato (Any other color will do.)
- 1 cup (150 g) diced green bell pepper (Any different

color will do.)

- ⅓ cup (5 g) loosely packed fresh cilantro leaves, minced
- ⅓ cup (20 g) minced scallion
- 1 small jalapeno, seeded and minced
- ⅓ teaspoon toasted cumin seeds
- Salt and pepper, optional
- Roasted pepitas (hulled pumpkin seeds), for garnish
- 1 lemon, cut into 4 to 6 wedges
- 1 lime, cut into 4 to 6 wedges

Instructions

1. Mix the couscous with the broth in a large glass bowl. Add the oil, lemon juice, and lime juice. Stir well. Cover and let stand 5 minutes until the liquids are absorbed. Fluff with a fork.

2. Add the beans, tomato, bell pepper, cilantro, scallion, and jalapeno on top. Rub the cumin seeds between your fingers while adding them to release the flavor. Fold to combine with a rubber spatula. Adjust the seasonings to taste. Refrigerate for at least 30 minutes to chill and to let the flavors meld.

3. Serve and garnish each portion with a small handful of pepitas and a wedge of lemon and lime to drizzle before eating.

4. Leftovers can be stored in an airtight container in the refrigerator for up to 4 days.

CURRIED BEAN AND CORN SALAD

Yield: 4 servings

Protein content per serving: 27 g

Ingredients

- Protein content per serving cup (90 g) whole freekeh
- 3 cups (705 ml) salted water
- 1 can (15 ounces, or 425 g) chickpeas, drained and rinsed
- 1 cup (164 g) fresh or frozen corn (run under hot water, drained)
- ¼ cup (40 g) minced red onion
- ¼ cup (32 g) minced celery
- ¼ cup (38 g) minced bell pepper (any color)

- 3 tablespoons (12 g) minced fresh parsley
- 1 tablespoon (6 g) curry powder (mild or hot)
- 1 teaspoon ground cumin
- 1 teaspoon garam masala
- 1teaspoon ginger powder
- 1teaspoon fine sea salt
- 1 clove garlic
- 2 tablespoons (30 ml) seasoned rice vinegar
- 3 tablespoons (45 ml) olive oil

Instructions

1. Bring the freekeh and salted water to a boil in a medium-size saucepan. Reduce to simmer and cook for 45 minutes, occasionally stirring, until tender. Drain and run under cold water, draining again. Transfer to a medium-size bowl. Add the chickpeas, corn, onion, celery, bell pepper, and parsley.

2. Heat the curry powder, cumin, and garam masala in a small skillet over medium heat. Stir and cook for 3 to 4 minutes until fragrant. Do not burn. Transfer to a small blender and add the ginger powder, salt, garlic, and vinegar. Blend until smooth. Add the olive oil and blend again to emulsify. Pour the dressing (to taste) over the bean mixture. Stir to coat and let sit for 15 minutes for the flavors to meld. The salad can also be covered and refrigerated for up to 3 days.

LEEK AND LEMON LENTIL SALAD

Yield: 4 servings

Protein Content Per Serving: 16 g

Ingredients

- 1 cup (192 g) dry French green lentils
- ¼ cup (60 ml) olive oil
- ⅔ cup (80 g) chopped leeks (white part only)
- 1 teaspoon dried thyme
- 2 cloves garlic, minced
- ¼ cup (60 ml) fresh lemon juice

- 1 teaspoon fine sea salt, or to taste
- Pinch of ground black pepper, or to taste
- 1 carrot, peeled, cut into quarters, then thinly sliced
- 6 small radishes, cut into quarters, then thinly sliced
- 2 small sunchokes, cut into quarters, then thinly sliced

Instructions

1. Bring a medium-size pot of water to a boil. Add the lentils. Reduce the heat to simmer. Cook for 25 to 30 minutes until tender. Drain and rinse with cold water. Drain again and then transfer to a medium-size bowl.

2. Heat the oil in a small skillet over medium heat. Add the leek and thyme. Cook, occasionally stirring, for 3 to 4 minutes until the leek is translucent. Add the garlic and cook for 1 minute longer. Transfer to a small blender. Add the lemon juice, salt, and pepper and process until smooth. Add the vegetables and dressing to the lentils. Stir to combine. Serve immediately or cover and refrigerate for up to 3 days. Taste and adjust the seasonings when serving.

EAT-IT-UP EDAMAME SALAD

cm) pieces of snow peas

- 1 cup (70 g) thinly sliced baby bok choy
- 1½ cup (27 g) minced scallion
- Protein content per serving cup (70 g) minced carrot
- 2 tablespoons (30 ml) seasoned rice vinegar
- 2 tablespoons (30 ml) tamari, or to taste
- 1 tablespoon (15 ml) vegetable broth
- 2 teaspoons ume plum vinegar
- 2 teaspoons toasted sesame oil
- Protein content per serving teaspoon sambal oelek, or to taste
- ¼ teaspoon minced garlic

- ¼ teaspoon grated fresh ginger root
- Salt and pepper

Instructions

1. Bring a large pot of water to boil. Add the edamame, somen, and salt. Cook for 2 minutes or until the noodles are soft but do not overcook.

2. Drain immediately and rinse under cold water until chilled, draining again. Combine the snow peas, baby bok choy, scallion, and carrot in a medium-size bowl. Add the somen and edamame to the vegetables.

3. Combine the rice vinegar, tamari, broth, ume plum vinegar, sesame oil, sambal oelek, garlic, and ginger in a small blender. Process until smooth. Pour over the salad and stir to coat. Cover and refrigerate for 1 hour, or longer for the flavors to meld. Taste and adjust the seasonings when serving.

CPSIA information can be obtained
at www.ICGtesting.com
Printed in the USA
BVHW092306140621
609528BV00010B/1412